Published by Akashic Books
All rights reserved
Words ©2024 Scott Woodruff and Adam Mansbach
Illustrations ©2024 Juan Manuel Orozco

ISBN: 978-1-63614-175-6
Library of Congress Control Number: 2023949477

First printing
Printed in China

Akashic Books
Instagram, X, Facebook: AkashicBooks
info@akashicbooks.com
www.akashicbooks.com

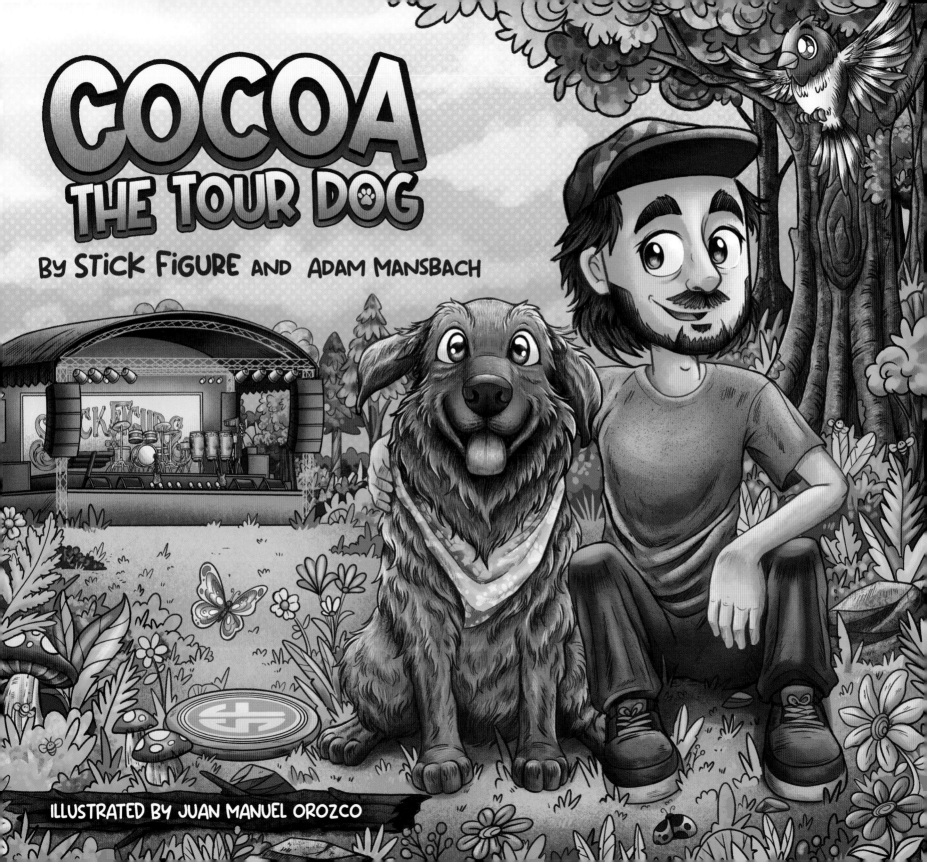

Our story begins on a day in late May,
In a place full of doggos who don't want to stay.
Alsatians, dalmatians, and oodles of poodles;
Pits, pugs, and huskies named Fitz, Muggs, and Dusty.
Some were young pups, some had beards salt-and-peppered,
And off in the corner—one Australian shepherd,

Wondering how long this place would be home,
Itching to run and to romp and to roam,
Through sand and sea foam with a friend of her own.
When suddenly—in walked some dude and said, "Her!
That beautiful pup with the chocolatey fur!"

The next thing she knew, he was calling her Cocoa.
He signed his name *Scott*, and then said, "Time to go, yo!"
The guy at the desk tried to hand him a leash,
But Scott told him, "No thanks, we don't need it. Peace!"
He looked down at Cocoa, as if to say, *Right?*
She wagged her bum *Yes* and walked into the night.

A few minutes later, they got to his place.
Scott glanced down and laughed at the look on her face.
"It's not much," he said, "I should probably clean it.
But you'll be loved here, and I surely do mean it."
This was a lot. Cocoa felt scared and shy.
She lay on a blanket and half closed one eye.

Scott sat beside her and picked up a thing,
And touched the thing's strings, and then started to sing.
Cocoa felt chills, and then warm happy tears.
Whatever *this* was, she was all ears.
And that was the start
Of the pair's happy years.

The Frisbee went sailing out over the waves,
And Cocoa ran so fast you wouldn't believe it.
She leaped past the breakers, so giddy and brave,
Then trotted to shore like, *No biggie, retrieved it.*

Scott took the Frisbee and sat in the sand,
And said, "I've got news about me and the band.
We finally managed to book a few shows.
And that means we have to go out on the road."
Cocoa was worried—would he leave her behind?
But Scott shook his head as if reading her mind,
And then rubbed her tummy and said, "You see,
When I say *we*—I mean *you and me*."

The sign on the door said, *All Dogs Must Be Leashed,*
The food in the green room was far from a feast.
It was time to perform, so Scott told her, "Chill here,"
But the green room was lonely and smelled like spilled beer.
So Cocoa decided to make a new choice
And follow the sound of her friend's singing voice.

ALL DOGS MUST
BE LEASHED

The next thing she knew—she was standing onstage;
A small crowd of people stared at her, amazed.
"Cocoa," Scott whispered, "can't you see that we're—"
Before he could finish, he was drowned by a cheer.
Scott winked at Cocoa; his next move was clear.
He yelled, "Cocoa the Tour Dog!" and grinned ear to ear.

The crowds grew and grew, through the band's perseverance,
And the highlight of each show was Cocoa's appearance.
One night, after playing a show that was packed,
They went to a restaurant for a late snack.
"Certainly not!" fumed the man at the door.
"No dogs are allowed to step foot on the floor!"

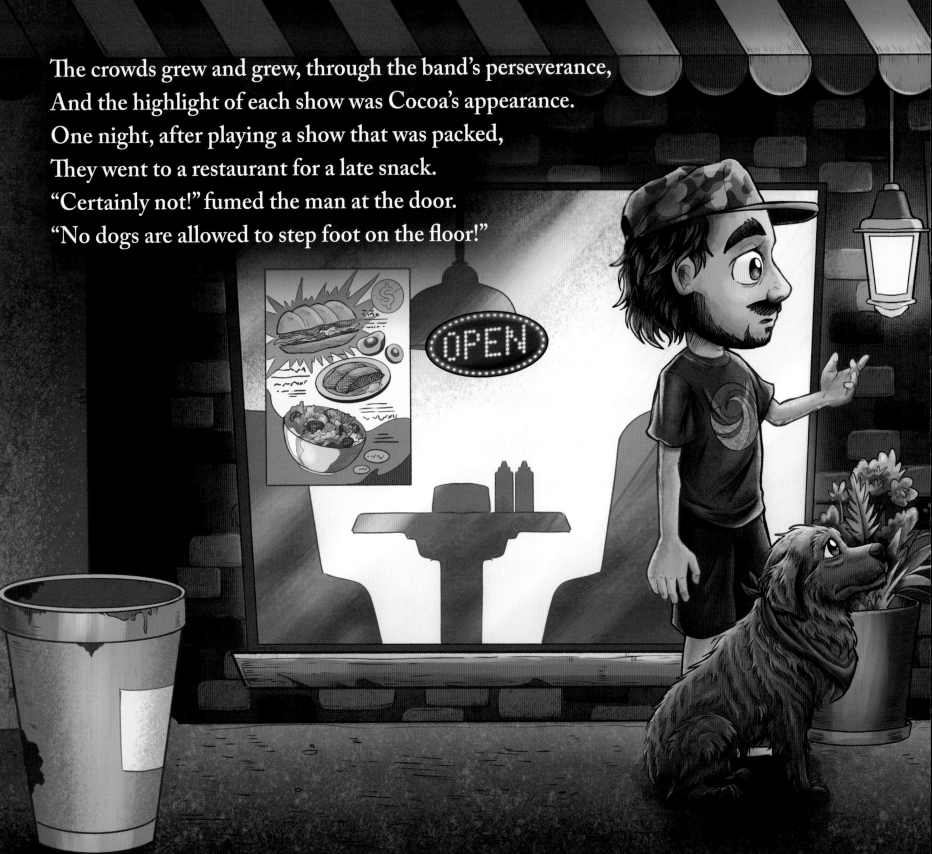

Just then, a couple of young music fans
Walked up and said, "It's that dog! From that band!
You're awesome! You're famous! Can we take a picture?
It's cool if your friend wants to get in it wit'cha!"
Cocoa and Scott posed; it didn't take long,
And after, the man sang a whole different song.

"Sorry," he said, "for that heartless rejection.
Since you are famous, we'll make an exception.
Come right this way, welcome one, welcome all!"

At the airport in London, it was pretty funny:
With no leash, Cocoa couldn't come into the country.
Scott mulled it over and said, "This is weird, but . . ."
And tied Cocoa's collar to one of his earbuds.

That night they played before thousands of people,
And when Cocoa came out, she felt special and regal.
Her name was on signs that the fans held aloft.
They threw toys onstage for her, furry and soft.
Bright lights exploded and lit up the night;
She took it all in, thinking, *This is the life*.

She never grew tired of touring with Scott,
or the joy the fans got when she walked in the spot,
Or the beach in the morning to see the sun rise;
Scott would hug her and say, "We're lucky guys."
But little by little, to Cocoa's surprise,
She stopped seeing everything through puppy eyes.

Sometimes, the grind of the road wore her down,
Or the meetings they had to take all over town.
Cocoa was simple; she didn't need much—
Just a swim in the sea and a Frisbee to clutch—
Not her face airbrushed on the side of a bus
That she sat in alone, full of stuffies so plush.

Things took a turn for the worse in Flagstaff;
All day long, Cocoa had signed pawtographs.
She lay on her bed in the bus, thinking fame
Was not nearly as fun as a run in the rain,
And sighed as she heard the crowd chanting her name.

But Cocoa didn't trot out to bask in the love,
She just sighed again and stayed right where she was.
It made her feel wretched, but she was so tired;
Alone on a bus, how could she feel inspired?

She could tell Scott was worried; back home the next day,
He woke her up early, said, "Ready to play?"
He grabbed his guitar: "It's beach time, Cocoa!"
But to her dismay, she could not find her mojo.
She'd left it in Soho, or maybe Kyoto
Or San Antonio? Tokyo? Acapulco?

"Guess you're not feeling it." Scott sounded so low.
He grabbed his guitar and walked to the beach solo.
Cocoa gave in to her aches and her blues
And settled herself for a long morning snooze.

When Cocoa woke up, Scott was back by her side.
Excitement danced deep in the blues of his eyes.
"Cocoa," he said, "come see what I found!"
The photo he showed her left Cocoa spellbound,
And her brain rewound to that day at the pound

When Scott had walked in the door, picked her and kissed her—
The pup in the picture could have been her sister.
"She's someplace called Serbia," Scott told her then.
"What do you think—time for a new friend?"
Cocoa gazed at her and thought of her plight,
And something inside her knew that it felt right.

To cross half the world took a day and a half,
With no band or bus, no roadies or staff.
Just Cocoa and Scott, just the way it had been,
Ready to welcome another one in.

When they got there, the pup danced around like a sprite
And nipped Cocoa's neck; it was love at first bite.
"Feels like fam to me," announced Scott with a laugh,
And when they left, he threw her leash in the trash.

Cocoa remembered this feeling so well;
She looked at the pup and she felt her heart swell.
Scott bent to give her a kiss and said, "Prolly
Should give her a name—what do you think of *Molly*?"

Cocoa barked *Yup* and then Molly did too,
And where there'd been two, now there was a crew.

From that moment on, life never was boring.
Cocoa taught her sister all about touring
And Frisbees and merch tables, buses and beaches,
And how to ignore all the rules about leashes.

Molly learned fast, she was playful and spry,
And Cocoa was seeing with new puppy eyes.
Soon there was only one thing left to do:
Bring Molly onstage to make her debut.

Cocoa and Scott thought it would be so stellar
To bring Mol' onstage the last night of Coachella.
But Molly was nervous, which was understandable—
It was a big deal for this sweet young animal.

So as the set ended and the chants began,
Cocoa explained that this family of fans
Felt the same love for Cocoa as she felt for them,
The same love that Scott felt; it bounced around when
He sang songs, or they played a game at the beach,
And each time it bounced it expanded its reach.

From Molly to Cocoa, from Cocoa to Scott,
The band, and the fans, and what they all got
Was a wonderful feeling of being a part
Of something much bigger—and this was the start.
Cocoa had planned to go on and say more,
But Molly was bounding straight for the stage door,
And when she stepped out and the crowd gave a roar,
Cocoa looked at Scott and felt her heart soar.
From a cage to the stage, they began a new tour.

STICK FIGURE, a band with a distinctive sound developed through tireless attention to musicality and artistry, has redefined American reggae music with their album *Wisdom*, released in September 2022. As with the band's previous releases, *Wisdom* was written, produced, and recorded by Scott Woodruff, a multi-instrumentalist and self-taught musician. *Wisdom* is the band's seventh album and follows the unprecedented success of 2019's *World on Fire*, with *Billboard* certifying Stick Figure as the top-selling living reggae artist every year since 2019. Scott began writing and recording songs at an early age, and what was once a hobby grew into a worldwide phenomenon.

ADAM MANSBACH is the author of a #1 *New York Times* best-selling, beloved, and bad-word-filled "children's book" that our publisher won't let us name here, as well as the novels *The Golem of Brooklyn, Rage Is Back, The End of the Jews*, and *Angry Black White Boy;* and the memoir-in-verse *I Had a Brother Once*. With Dave Barry and Alan Zweibel, he coauthored *For This We Left Egypt?* and the best-selling *A Field Guide to the Jewish People*. Mansbach's books for young readers include the *New York Times* bestseller *Just Try One Bite* and the award-winning Jake the Fake series.

JUAN MANUEL OROZCO is a graphic artist and illustrator from Costa Rica, recognized as the official visual artist for Stick Figure since 2018. He is also known for his work with Metallica and the Dave Matthews Band, among other top-tier clients and art projects.